Flight Zero One

by

Tony Breeze

CHARACTERS

Judy Robinson	Female pilot with small Canadian airline, a rough & ready survivor
Bill & Mary McMurdo	Sickly old man (NS) & his wife who've been together through thick & thin
Tasmin Archer & Joe	Heavily pregnant young woman & her partner, tomorrow's young hopefuls
Mrs Hooper & Abigail	Mother & precocious daughter on their way to a TV audition
Walter J.Cronkheim III	Grumpy businessman on his way to his next buck
Vanessa James	Fading actress on her way to a facelift
Officer Sharpe	A Canadian policeman on his way to court with the Red Indian
Officer Mulligan	Female police officer also acting as escort.
Sammy Two-Rivers	Red Indian prisoner on his way to court; slow, charismatic, a man of few words

(Introductory music Sinatra's "Come Fly With Me" - music down – sound of wind howling. We see the dark and dusty interior of a Canadian fur trapper's cabin in winter.

Voices off	"Over there, there's a cabin, etc.

(We hear someone trying to open the old door but it won't budge)

Judy	(Off) The door's jammed.
Joe	Here, let me try

(The rickety door is eventually forced open and a group of people come in with a flashlight. They are not dressed for the snow but have airline blankets wrapped round them to keep them warm)

Cronkheim	(Carrying holdall) Jesus H. Christ! Don't ever do that to me again
Judy	(Shining flashlight around) What's wrong? I got you down didn't I?
Cronkheim	You got us down - you certainly did that, babe.
Vanessa	I've never been so frightened in all my life.
Mrs Hooper	Everybody told me I shouldn't fly at New Year.

3

Mary McM	(Supporting her elderly husband) Come in, love, you'll be all right now
Mrs Hooper	I want you to know that I'll be making a formal complaint to the airline about this
Abigail	(To her mum) Don't fuss me -
Mrs Hooper	She nearly got us killed
Joe	(Bringing in heavily pregnant wife) If you must know, she actually saved your lives - if she hadn't found that clearing when she did, we'd have been spread over three states
Judy	Thank you. You think that I did it on purpose? That I arranged for the engines to develop problems?
Mrs Hooper	I've never prayed so much in my whole life - they were right about it being unlucky to fly at this time of year.
Judy	It was nothing to do with the time of year, it was probably just dirt in the fuel line.
Vanessa	Whatever. We're here now, safe and well, which is more than I thought we'd be ten minutes ago
	(Two police officers bring in a prisoner in handcuffs who looks as if he's from Indian stock)
Sharpe	Come on in, son, make yourself at home

(Everyone stops and looks as the Indian slowly walks across the room)

Mulligan   Sit yourself down over there - and no funny business.

Joe   (To his pregnant wife) Are you all right love?

Tasmin   I think so.

Joe   Come and sit down (he takes her to a chair)

Vanessa   "It ain't much but its home" ... what _is_ this place?

Sharpe   It's what the fur trappers used to use in the old days

Vanessa   (Running her finger along dust) You'd think they'd at least clean the place up before they left, it's filthy

Cronkheim   Maam, the temperature outside is minus thirty, we've just escaped death by inches and between you and me I don't give a shit about the dust

Mrs Hooper   Hey! Watch your language.

Vanessa   There's a stove and some lamps!

Joe   All we got to do is find a way of lighting them. Anybody got a light?

(They all look at each other and shake their heads)

Cronkheim	Wouldn't you just know it - not only do I crash-land in the middle of nowhere but I'm stuck in a freezing cabin with a bunch of schmucks who don't have a match between them
Joe	Come on, somebody must have a light - my wife's pregnant
Cronkheim	You don't say? And here was I thinking it was the warm bread she'd been eating
Joe	(To Judy) You must have something to make a fire
Judy	We've got plenty of kerosene in the plane, you almost had all the fire you wanted back there.
Joe	You officer, do you have a light?
Sharpe	I'm afraid I don't smoke
Joe	(To Mulligan) What about you?
Mulligan	(Shaking head) Sorry
Joe	Does he?
Sharpe	He's not allowed
Joe	Somebody must have one

Cronkheim   The trick is to conserve energy, I've seen it in the movies. All we've got to do is snuggle down together till daylight and in the morning we can get out of here

Vanessa   If you think I'm snuggling down with you, you've got another thing coming

Sharpe   (To Indian who is moving towards stove) Where d'you think you're going?

Mulligan   (Hand on her gun) What are you doing?

    (The Indian doesn't speak but, still handcuffed, gathers some rubbish from the floor, puts it in the stove and when he moves away we see it bursting into flames. The others cheer & keep the fire going by putting bits on)

Vanessa   Hey! We got a fire!

Cronkheim   That's great, son. How did you do that? Old Indian secret?

    (The Indian doesn't speak but holds up a cigarette lighter which he flicks into life and smiles)

Sharpe   You shouldn't have that – give it here. (He takes it off him and gives it to the young Joe who begins to light the oil lamps.

    (To Mulligan) I thought you said you'd searched him?

Mulligan   I did.

Cronkheim	What's he in for?
Sharpe	Arson.
Cronkheim	Great ... he doesn't say a lot does he?
	(The Indian gives him a disdainful look)
Vanessa	So what's the plan Miss Erhart?
Judy	The plan is to try and keep warm till morning, then when first light comes we see where we go from there
Cronkheim	Can't you get a message out on the radio in the plane?
Judy	It went down when we landed
Vanessa	I'm not surprised, my heart went down with it.
Tasmin	I'll try my mobile (she tries to dial but fails) Wouldn't you just know it – no signal
Judy	We're too far away from any transmitters.
Abigail	Mom, I'm hungry
Mrs. Hooper	I know dear. Mommy will sort something out
	(She turns to Cronkheim and speaks as if expecting action)
	My daughter's hungry.

Cronkheim   Is that so? And just what d'you think I'm gonna do about it?

Mrs Hooper   You could go into the woods - catch a rabbit or something

Cronkheim   Are you serious?

Mrs Hooper   Sure

Cronkheim   I don't like to say this, Maam, but the snow out there is four feet thick - if you think I'm freezing my balls off chasing conies in the middle of the night so your kid can fill her fat face, you've got another thing coming ... She looks as if she might just have enough reserves to last her till morning.

Mrs Hooper   Well!

Abigail   (Pointedly to Cronkheim) I don't like you.

Cronkheim   You know what kid? The feeling's completely mutual

Mary McM   I don't think my husband's very well

Judy   (Taking him to the second wooden bed) Come and lie down over here ... that's it

Mary McM   It's his heart ... he's had trouble before ... we were on the way to see our kids for the New Year but with all the excitement ...

Judy	He'll be OK ... just try and keep him warm. I'll go and look for some wood
	(She exits with difficulty through the rickety door)
Tasmin	Are you letting her go out on her own?
Cronkheim	I sure am
Tasmin	But there might be grizzly bears out there
Cronkheim	Precisely
Tasmin	(To Joe) You go, love
Joe	What about you?
Tasmin	I'll be OK
Joe	If you're sure
	(He follows her out, also struggling with the door)
Mulligan	(Following them) I'll give them a hand
Vanessa	(To Cronkheim) Have you no shame?
Cronkheim	You got it (meaning 'dead right')
Sharpe	I'd have gone but there's no way I can leave this guy on his own

Vanessa	(Looking scathingly at Cronkheim) So much for gallant Canadian gentlemen
Cronkheim	Maam, I ain't Canadian and I sure as hell ain't no gentleman
Vanessa	This is the last time I fly this airline
Cronkheim	It was nearly the last time you flew any airline - if she hadn't spotted that clearing we'd've been singing with the heavenly choir
Tasmin	Should we send somebody out to get help?
Cronkheim	By my estimation the nearest help is Fort Vermilion, about a hundred miles that away (Points with thumb) You gonna start walking? Don't forget it's New Year's Eve - would you be out in the back of beyond at this time of year if you didn't have to be?

(They shake their heads)

The whole damn world is either gathered round their TV sets or partying the night away

Mrs Hooper	Some New Year we're gonna have.
Cronkheim	God, it feels even colder in here than it is outside

(Pause while they all take in their plight)

Vanessa	So why don't we have our own here?

Mrs Hooper   Our own what?

Vanessa   Party - to warm us up, boost our morale

Cronkheim   Am I hearing you right? You almost met your maker out there and now you want to party?

Vanessa   Why not?

Cronkheim   Who're you going to invite? Santa Claus?

Vanessa   (Indicating others) We got all the guests we need right here

(Judy, Joe & Mulligan struggle back in with kindling)

Judy   What for?

Vanessa   I think what we need is a party

Judy   Yeah?

Vanessa   Yeah - right here and now - there ain't no reason to be miserable, just 'cos we've had a little setback - this is New Years Eve

Cronkheim   'Setback' she calls it. We belly-flop in the middle of nowhere and she calls it a "setback" - is she real?

Vanessa   Where's your spirit?

Cronkheim	I got all the spirit I need right here in this bag (Producing a bottle of whiskey from his bag) Never travel anywhere without it
Vanessa	I wasn't exactly thinking of that sort but it'll do for starters.
Cronkheim	What d'you mean?
Judy	There's some mugs over there (she goes for them)
Cronkheim	Who said I was sharing it?
Vanessa	Sure you'll share it - you wouldn't be that mean
Cronkheim	Wouldn't I?
Judy	I'm afraid they're a bit dusty
Vanessa	(To Cronkheim) Come on
Cronkheim	Aw!
	(He reluctantly hands it over for the common good and she begins to pour)
Abigail	(Prissily) What am I going to drink?
Mrs Hooper	Do you want mommy to get you some snow to melt?
Abigail	Yuk! No thanks
Joe	I've got something she can have (produces a carton of juice from his bag)

Cronkheim	Didn't you send out a mayday or whatever it is you're supposed to do?
Judy	There wasn't time
Abigail	We could light a signal fire outside
Mrs Hooper	It would take too long dear - we'll be OK in here
Judy	Come and get it

(They go for the mugs of whiskey)

Tasmin	(To Joe) Not for me, you go ahead
Mulligan	This ain't so bad - we got a stove, we got some lamps and we got this
Vanessa	Yeah, but where are we gonna sleep?
Cronkheim	(Sitting on the spare bed) I bags this bed
Vanessa	If you had anything about you, you'd give it up for somebody more deserving
Cronkheim	There ain't anybody more deserving than me
Sharpe	(Approaching him and towering over him) I really think you ought to consider the young lady, sir

(Cronkheim sees that he means what he says and backs down)

Cronkheim	(Moving) Of course - I wasn't serious

(We end up with the old man on one side of the stage and pregnant young woman in a bed on the other)

Vanessa   I know what this party's lacking - we don't know anything about the other guests - so how's about we all introduce ourselves?

(Murmur from the others)

I'll start the ball rolling since it was my idea - I guess you all know me?

(They all shake their heads murmuring "No," etc)

But you must do - don't you watch TV?

Abigail   You've been on TV?

Vanessa   I want you to look very carefully

(She gives a side view)

How about this side?

Abigail   Sorry

Mrs Hooper   (Hesitantly) You do seem a little familiar

Vanessa   There you go

Mrs Hooper   You weren't on that quiz show where they - ?

Vanessa   No! I wasn't on any quiz show

15

Mary McM	(Matter-of-factly) You're the woman with the dog
Mrs Hooper	The what?
Mary McM	In the commercial, the woman that's waiting at the bus stop when she gets peed on by the dog
Vanessa	Well actually -
Mrs Hooper	Yes I know the one - you're her?
Vanessa	I wouldn't call it the pinnacle of my career - but yes, that was me
Abigail	Yeah, that's a great one
Vanessa	(To herself) Thirty years in the business and I'm remembered for being peed on by a dog!
Mrs Hooper	It's a good commercial - I watch that one - some of the others I don't bother with but that one I do
Vanessa	I'm greatly honoured
Abigail	What was the dog called?
Vanessa.	(Tetchily) I don't remember what the damned dog was called!
Mrs Hooper	Have you done anything else?
Vanessa	Of course ... nothing much recently ... but I'm waiting on one or two things

Mrs Hooper	Do you hear that? She's a real actress (to Vanessa) My daughter wants to go into show business - we're actually on the way to an audition for the Hughie Mortimer Show right now
Vanessa	(Again disdainfully) Really?
Mrs Hooper	Show them, Abigail
Vanessa	No, really

(But Abigail needs no further encouragement - she takes up a pose and begins singing the Lion's song from the Wizard of Oz 'If I only had a heart' [or some other audition piece]. All the others wince visibly and Abigail doesn't know when to stop. When she does there is muted applause)

Judy	(Interrupting at appropriate moment and sounding unconvincing) That's great
Mrs Hooper	She hasn't finished yet
Cronkheim	(Loud stage whisper) If I only had a gun!
Mrs Hooper	(Casting a nasty look at Cronkheim) (To others) Well what d'you think?
Mulligan	(Sounding unconvincing) She's very good
Abigail	Should I do some more?

Vanessa	(Quickly) No dear, that's great, we want to hear from some of the others
	(She indicates Judy)
Judy	Well you all know me, I'm the one that got you into this mess - Judy's the name - spent most of my life spraying crops and dousing forest fires till I got this job - that's about all there is for me
Sharpe	We don't blame you, maam
Cronkheim	I do. If the plane had been properly serviced none of this would have happened
Vanessa	So what's your claim to fame?
Cronkheim	I don't have one - Walter J Cronkheim the third at your service - I'm what you might call 'an entrepreneur'
Abigail	What's that mom?
Mrs Hooper	Somebody who makes money out of other people's misfortunes
Cronkheim	Don't pay your mom no heed, I just buy and sell things
Abigail	What do you buy?
Cronkheim	I buy what one person doesn't want and sell it to somebody who does

Abigail	Why doesn't the second one just miss you out and buy it themselves from the first one?
Cronkheim	Because he sometimes doesn't know he needs it till I convince him that he does – it's called the power of persuasion
Vanessa	(Disdainfully) It's called capitalism
	(Abigail looks confusedly at her mom who fobs her off with a wave of the hand)
Abigail	What if the second one doesn't want what the first one's got?
Cronkheim	Then we have to resort to something to make him think he needs it – good old advertising
Judy	(To young couple) What about you two?
Joe	We were hoping to get to Edmonton - my wife has to see a specialist there - (nodding towards her swollen abdomen) We lost our first kiddy (thinking what he's said he tries to backtrack) but I'm sure we'll be OK this time
Vanessa	Sure you will... (Turning to prisoner and Sharpe) Say, is this guy dangerous?
Sharpe	I don't reckon so, Maam
Mulligan	He aint given us any trouble so far.
Mrs Hooper	Shouldn't you go and sit in the plane with him

Judy   I don't think there's any need for that, it's freezing out there - if the man says he's not dangerous, we'll take his word for it

Mrs Hooper   I shan't sleep

Cronkheim   You'll sleep all right

Mrs Hooper   What about my daughter?

Cronkheim   He'll be quite safe from her

Mrs Hooper   Charming!

Judy   He doesn't mean it

Cronkheim   Don't I?

Mulligan   (To the old lady) Are you O.K.?

Mary McM   I don't know. We were hoping to get to Calgary to see our kids but it doesn't look like we'll make it now.

Mulligan   You'll make it all right, but not tonight.

Judy   (To others) O.K. So now we all know each other a little better how's about we find out what provisions we've got between us.

Mrs Hooper   Provisions?

Judy   Yeah, food

Mrs Hooper   We don't have any food

Abigail   I wish we did.

Judy   Somebody must have something

Mary McM   (Going to her bag) I have an apple pie that I was taking for the family. I don't mind if you folks want to share it between you.

Judy   (Taking it from her) That's very kind of you ... anybody else?

Joe Archer   We got a little chocolate you can have

Judy   O.K., let's have it for the communal store

Vanessa   I got some boiled sweets

Judy   Pass 'em over.

Sharpe   We've got a couple of sandwiches left I think – (checks his bag) Yeah, there you go.

Judy   (To Cronkheim) What about you?

Cronkheim   What about me.

Judy   You got any kind of eatables?

Cronkheim   I might have

Vanessa   What does that mean?

Cronkheim   It means, "What I got is none of your business"

Judy   Mister, we got ourselves into a predicament here and the only way we're going to get out if safe and sound is to share out fairly all we got.

Cronkheim   Why should I have to suffer just because you lot didn't have the foresight to think ahead.

Joe   You got some stuff in that bag?

Cronkheim   (Putting his arm round it) What's it to you?

Mulligan   I think you should hand it over, friend

Cronkheim   (Guarding his bag) Why should I? Why should I have to do without?

Joe   You wouldn't be so mean

Cronkheim   You just watch me

(At this point the Indian gets up and walks slowly over to Cronkheim who is clutching his beloved bag. The Indian takes hold of the bag and roughly drags it from his grasp then takes it to the centre and tips out his goodies and belongings into the middle, throwing down the bag and giving Cronkheim one of his looks)

Cronkheim   Hey ! That's theft. That's my property. You've no right.

Judy	We got every right. (She begins to share it out with the others) Here you are – make the most of it - I don't know when we'll be eating again.
All	(As she goes round them) Thanks, etc
Vanessa	This guy reckons we're a hundred miles from civilisation. Is he right?
Judy	I'm afraid so
Mrs Hooper	So how long do you reckon we'll have to stay here?
Judy	I don't rightly know
Sharpe	At some stage, when they realise we haven't arrived they'll start looking for us.
Mulligan	Especially the people who were waiting for Sammy, here
Mrs Hooper	But we're not in any kind of danger?
Cronkheim	Just depends what you call danger. If the weather comes down we could be here a long while. I heard a case where a plane came down like this in the mountains and the folks got so hungry they ended up having to eat the bodies of them that had been killed.
Abigail	Ugh!
Mrs Hooper	Will you please stop frightening my daughter like that. (To others) I'm sure he does it on purpose.

Judy   I don't think there's any need to worry about things like that. There's got to be some kind of settlement hereabouts with a landline

(Pause)

O.K. Now we've all had a little something to eat I reckon we should try and settle down and get some rest. we'll need all the energy we can muster in the morning.

All   Yeah, OK, good idea, goodnight, etc

(As they settle down they turn down the oil lamps and the stage lights go dimmer at the same time)

(Pause)

Vanessa   Excuse me officer, what time do you make it?

Sharpe   Half after eleven

Mrs Hooper   (Indicating stove) Can't you get any more heat out of that thing?

Judy   I'll try (she puts more wood on)

Cronkheim   They'll all be gathering now in Times Square

Mulligan   You from New York?

Cronkheim   Yes Maam .... The Big Apple.

Mulligan   I suppose you miss all the razzamatazz?

Cronkheim	To tell you the God's honest truth, I hate the whole goddam business - all that false bonhomie
Vanessa	Don't you like New Year?
Cronkheim	Why should I? Every year's the same ... The partying and the tinsel ... "Happy new year!" ... all that kissing and hugging and Christ knows what ... and the resolutions ... 'I will be good to the wife' ... "I'll give up smoking" ... "I'll be nice to my husband" ... and what happens? Next morning when the fog clears they're right back at each other's throats – it's a load of old hogwash!
Mrs Hooper	Don't you think it brings out the best in people?
Cronkheim	I'll tell you something, lady, when they reach the next millennium, though I won't be there, things will still be the same - human nature never changes - they'll still be robbing each other, chasing their secretaries, fornicating, wanting what the other person's got - I tell you nothing changes
Abigail	What's 'fornicating'?
Mrs Hooper	Never you mind - you should be asleep
Abigail	(Getting up) I can't sleep
Mrs Hooper	Where are you going?
Abigail	To put some more wood on the stove

(She does so, prodding and poking at it)

Judy (Going to the elderly couple) How is he?

Mary McM He feels cold - he keeps asking if we're there yet. I don't think he knows where we are

Judy Does he take any tablets or anything?

Mary McM He does but they're all used up

Judy (To everyone) Is there anyone here with any medical training?

(General 'no,' 'sorry,' etc but the Indian slowly gets up and with his hands still tethered walks over and views the state of the old man, puts his hand on the old man's neck then walks back to Sharpe and whispers something to him)

Judy What's he say?

Sharpe He says you're wasting your time - he thinks the old man's time has come

Judy Yeah? Well what does he know? (To the Indian) You a trained medic? Eh?

(No reply)

Mulligan I've done a little first aid

Judy (Waving towards old man) Could you just ....

Mulligan Sure

(She goes across to try and help, taking his pulse. etc)

Abigail   (Going to Indian) You a real Indian?

Mrs Hooper   Abigail!   What are you doing?

Abigail   Just talking to him

Mrs Hooper   Come here

Abigail   It's OK mom, he wont hurt me

              (To Sharpe) What did he do?

Sharpe   Some men did something to bad his wife so he followed them up north and when he found out where they were living, they say he tied up the doors of their cabin and set fire to it – but he don't agree with that version – says he wants to go to court so he can tell them how it really happened but I don't know whether to believe him.

Abigail   (To Indian) Did you really set fire to that cabin?

              (He doesn't answer her)

              (To Sharpe) Are you sure he can talk?

Sharpe   Yeah he can talk - when he feels like it

Cronkheim   He must be great company

Mulligan   (Anxiously to Judy) Excuse me Miss but -

Judy   (Going across) What's wrong?

Mulligan   (Casting a glance towards the old man) I think ...

                (Judy frantically checks the old man and begins
                heart massage)

Judy   (To Mulligan) Don't just stand there!

                (Mulligan tries mouth-to-mouth while the Judy
                continues the heart massage. All the others
                gather round murmuring except Cronkheim, the
                Indian, Mrs Hooper and Abigail)

Judy   (Eventually giving up) It's no good

Mary McM   (Matter-of-factly) He's gone hasn't he?

Mulligan   I'm afraid so

                (Beat)

                (Vanessa comforts the old lady)

Cronkheim   I guess your friend knows more than he lets on

Mrs Hooper   You mean he just died on us? Right here?

Cronkheim   Some people have no consideration.

Mrs Hooper   What're we gonna do?

Judy   About what?

Mrs Hooper   (Putting her arms protectively round daughter) We can't just sit here with a ... a ...

Cronkheim   "Body's" the word you're looking for

Judy   We'll have to take him out to the plane

Cronkheim   Why don't you just bury him outside?

Judy   Don't be so heartless (To others) Will some of you give us a hand?

(Joe & Sharpe help Judy to remove the body in a blanket. They struggle again with the sticking door and the old lady tearfully follows them out)

Cronkheim   Some party this turned out to be ... well he didn't quite make it to the New Year

(He goes over to where the old man was lying and picks up the unused mug of whiskey)

He won't be needing this any more (raises the mug to the Vanessa before drinking it) Good health! (He drinks)

This trip is getting more like an Agatha Christie novel every minute – I reckon I should open a book on who's gonna be next to go

Vanessa   With your sense of humour it could be you

Abigail   Where's the old lady going, mom?

Mrs Hooper	I think s she's going to stay in the plane with the ... er ... with her husband. They'll probably give her something to keep her warm.
Abigail	(Childishly interested) This has been really cool. It's the first time I've ever seen somebody really die.
Mrs Hooper	Yes dear
Abigail	I mean you see it in the movies and on TV but that's the first time I've ever seen an actual body
Cronkheim	You do that Shirley Temple stuff again and you might just see another
Mrs Hooper	I beg your pardon?
Cronkheim	You heard
Mrs Hooper	How dare you insult my daughter in front of me
Cronkheim	I'm sorry, I didn't realise it was your turn. So what would you like me to say?

(The two of them by now are nose to nose)

Mrs Hooper	I've just about had enough of you and your wise cracking
Cronkheim	You ain't heard nothing yet, lady
Mrs Hooper	Ever since we left you've done nothing but complain

Cronkheim   So tell me - how come you have to get your kicks by shoving your daughter into show biz?

Mrs Hooper   You what?

Cronkheim   It's a well known fact the only reason mothers push their kids into show business is because they couldn't do it themselves when they were young

Mrs Hooper   How dare you!

(Abigail begins to cry)

Now look what you've done

(The others struggle back through the door carrying wood for the fire)

Judy   What's going on?

Mulligan   Our friend here has been exercising his charms again

Cronkheim   What's the big deal? I only told the truth, the kid's useless - somebody ought to tell her - she either learns now or she learns later

(This prompts more walling from Abigail and a general melee begins to develop with everyone arguing except the young couple and the Indian)

(The following are intermingled and ad-libbed to create a general hubbub)

Judy	I wish you'd keep your comments to yourself
Cronkheim	Why should I? I'm entitled to speak my mind
Sharpe	I must admit he's got a point, she isn't very good
Vanessa	She's not exactly the greatest singer I've ever heard but ...
Abigail	You're all being really horrible to me!

(Joe who has been tending his wife emerges through the arguing throng carrying a small transistor radio to his ear and stops them all in mid flow)

Joe	Hey everybody! Do you know what time it is? It's almost here - the New Year!

(They stop and he turns up the volume on the radio - we hear the end of the chiming of midnight from a city clock followed by a crowd heartily singing Auld Lang Syne)

Vanessa	Happy New Year!
All	Happy New Year!

(They all go round hugging each other except Cronkheim who fobs them off with a wave of his hand. The Indian too keeps himself to himself)

Cronkheim	Thank God that's all over, perhaps now we can get some sleep

Vanessa	It's too early to sleep, the party's only just begun
Cronkheim	Some party
Abigail	We don't have any jelly or ice cream
Cronkheim	We got plenty of ice.
Mrs Hooper	But no cream. The lady's right, it's too early to go to sleep. We need to do something
Abigail	We should play some party games.
Cronkheim	Include me out.
Sharpe	What we need are some stories to pass the time
Vanessa	Good idea. So who's got a story for the New Year?
	(They all shake their heads in turn)
	Come on, someone must have a story they can tell
All	No ... not me .. sorry .. I can't think of one, etc
Cronkheim	(Coming forward) I got a story
Vanessa	You?
Cronkheim	Yeah me. Don't look so surprised. Well do you want to hear it or don't you?

Abigail   Course we do

(They all settle down with Cronkheim holding the floor)

Cronkheim   When you're all ready ... This story came back to me because of where we are. It was told to me when I was a kid by my granddaddy and I've got no reason to believe it isn't true.

It's about two trappers who used to go north every year hunting for beaver and ended up living in a place just like this. They would spend the whole of the winter in the cabin, trapping during the day and talking and drinking all night. These fellahs were the best of pals, they'd gone to school together, known each other for years and got on really well – I was gonna say "like a house on fire" but thought better of it in the present company (they look at Sharpe and the Indian)

Then one day they were out tending to their traps when they came across a set of tracks in the snow that took them by surprise. These weren't just any old tracks - they looked like a set of human footprints, the sort of prints they'd never seen before in their lives. They were like the bare feet of a man but like no man they'd ever seen – they were huge – bigger than anything they'd ever seen and as they were looking at them the hairs on their neck started to stand on end and they got to feeling kind of scared, like they was being watched so they decided to hightail it back to their cabin and locked and bolted all the doors.

You never saw two men as spooked as they were ... they'd heard stories about the abominable snowman but like everybody else they'd just dismissed them all as foolish speculation ... so they got into their sleeping bags and tried to get to sleep but it wasn't easy. Eventually they settled down for the night and later on, when it was quiet, they began to hear what sounded like scratching noises outside the door of the cabin. One of them said he couldn't take it no more and that he was going outside with his gun to investigate and the other told him to stay where he was but he wouldn't be told and out he went into the freezing cold night with his rifle to see what was going on.

The guy that was left in the cabin listened for a while then after what seemed an eternity with only the sound of his heart thumping, he heard a gunshot and a scream, a horrible scream like nothing he'd ever heard before and his blood ran cold and it was then ... it was then that he heard something at the door of the cabin trying to get in...

(They are then disturbed themselves by a noise at the door of their own cabin)

Vanessa   (Jumping nervously) What's that?

Mrs Hooper   What's what?

Vanessa   (Scared) There's something at the door

Mulligan   Don't be silly

Vanessa   I did - I definitely heard something

Mrs Hooper   You're just jumpy because of the story

Vanessa   I'm not.

Mrs Hooper   Then go and look

Vanessa   I ain't opening it, it might be a grizzly

Abigail   Or the abominable snowman!

                (The door rattles again)

Vanessa   Now do you believe me?

                (They all look between each other)

Mrs Hooper   (To Sharpe) You go - you've got a gun

Sharpe   (Hesitating) This wouldn't stop a grizzly

                (The door rattles again)

Mrs Hooper   (Putting arms round daughter) For God's sake,
                somebody do something.

                (All are afraid to move except for the Indian who
                senses their fear and still in handcuffs he picks up
                a piece of firewood and slowly moves towards
                the door. On reaching it there is a dramatic pause
                as he looks back at the others then with great
                difficulty he yanks it open and raises the wood -

in comes Mrs McMurdo who has decided to leave the body of her husband in the plane)

Mary McM   (Standing in the doorway) The door wouldn't open - why are you all looking at me like that?

(Before anyone can reply they are interrupted by Tasmin)

Tasmin   (Holding her tummy) Oh no!

Vanessa   What is it?

Tasmin   (Crying with pain) Aah!

Joe   (Taking her towards the bed) Over here

(The lights go down again and when they come up we see everyone gathered round the bed but the woman's head is nearest the audience, her knees raised, so we witness the impending birth from the reaction in the faces of the onlookers. Mrs Hooper and Abigail, the Indian and Cronkheim keep themselves separate)

Vanessa   Come on, love, one last push (The woman is panting)

             That's it, great

Joe   Will she be OK?

Judy   Sure she will

Joe   I feel so helpless

Cronkheim   (Sarcastic) You've done your bit son

Mulligan   (To Cronkheim) You're not joining in Mr Cronkheim?

Cronkheim   No way

Judy   (To Cronkheim) You're not looking very well

Cronkheim   I hate this kind of thing - I think I need some air

              (He exits)

Abigail   (To Judy) Why does it hurt her so much?

Judy   Don't ask me, it's not something I've ever tried

Abigail   I don't think I'll bother

Vanessa   (To Tasmin) Almost there - come on then, one more push

              (Tasmin screams in agony)

Joe   What's wrong? There's something wrong!

              (There's a moment's panic while they look at each other not knowing what to do. The Indian who has kept himself separate from events walks calmly over, assesses the situation and still wearing the handcuffs bends down to help the trapped baby, eventually managing to help it out – we here it cry and everyone cheers)

Joe   Thank God!

Judy   (To Indian) You're a man of many parts mister - don't what we'd have done without you

      (He doesn't reply)

      (To Sharpe) Don't you think you ought to take the cuffs off him?

Sharpe   Not allowed, Maam

Mulligan Not unless we want to get put on a charge.

Joe   (Rushing to shake the Indian's hand) I don't care what you're supposed to have done, friend, I want to thank you

      (To Sharpe) Can't you give him a chance? Let him have an hour's start on you? We wouldn't tell anyone

Sharpe   More than my life's worth, I'm afraid

      (Cronkheim returns)

Cronkheim Is it safe yet?

Vanessa It's safe - she's had a little girl

Judy   Thanks to the Indian

Cronkheim I told you that guy's smarter than he looks - now you're gonna have to name it after his squaw

(Angry look from the Indian)

Sharpe   I shouldn't say that, sir, in their language "squaw" means 'loose woman'

Cronkheim   Begging your pardon, I'm sure

Abigail   What's a - ?

Mrs Hooper   Don't even ask

Vanessa   This demands a toast - everybody charge your glasses - I mean 'mugs'

(They do so)

A toast to the new baby - to - (she realises she hasn't got a name and shouts to Joe) What're you gonna call her?

Joe   We hadn't thought

Abigail   You should call her 'Ann'

Vanessa   Why Ann?

Abigail   Short for "Anno Domini!"

(Groans from the others)

Vanessa   It'll do for a working title - so everybody, (raising her mug) here's to Ann!

All   To Ann!

Mrs Hooper	Hang on, in all the excitement we've forgotten the really important thing about New Year
Judy	What's that?
Mrs Hooper	The resolutions. We haven't had any New Year resolutions yet - come on now, let's do this right - everybody has to think of something that they're going to try and do in the coming year - and it can't be something easy, it's got to be something you'll find really hard
Judy	That's easy for me then - I'm gonna resolve never to have to land in any forest clearings ever again

(Laughter)

Vanessa	(Turning to Cronkheim) Your turn
Cronkheim	I don't play party games
Vanessa	You've got to, don't be an old stick-in-the-mud
Cronkheim	Why should I?
Sharpe	Mister, my friend here is looking at you and when he does that it ain't a good sign
Cronkheim	OK, OK. You say it's got to be something I find hard to do? O.K - I'll give you a resolution – from now on I'm gonna try and think before I open my big mouth - how's that?
All	Yeah! You'll never do it, etc

Abigail	If that's the case I think perhaps mine should be to go to singing lessons

(Laughter)

Mrs Hooper	Perhaps Mr Cronkheim's right, perhaps I am too pushy
Vanessa	I'm gonna give up appearing on commercials
Mary McM	I think I'm going to try and spend a little more time with my grandchildren
Sharpe	I can't think of anything that we have any real problems with

(They look at the Indian who says nothing but he slips his hand out of one of the handcuffs to the amazement of Sharpe & Mulligan and points to the loose cuff with the free hand - laughter from others. The officers quickly go to refasten it)

Judy	It's getting kind of late and if we're going to get out of here tomorrow we'll need to be on the ball, so if you don't mind, I think it's time we tried to get some sleep.
Mrs Hooper	How can we sleep with all this talk of abominable snowmen and people eating bodies.
Judy	You're just going to have to try
Mrs Hooper	(To daughter) Come on, dear.

Vanessa	And no snoring Mr Cronkheim.
Cronkheim	What makes you think I snore?
Vanessa	You just look the type.
Cronkheim	Now I've heard everything (chunters to himself).
Judy	You can cuddle up to me, Mrs McMurdo, to keep warm
Mrs McM	Thank you dear.
Judy	(To the new parents who are holding the baby) Are you three OK?
Joe	You bet.
Tasmin	Did you thank the Indian guy for me?
	(Pause - then from the silence we here a deep booming voice)
Sammy	No problem.
Cronkheim	Good God! He spoke! He actually spoke.
	(Chuckles from the others)
	(The lights go down again to show a further passage of time. From this point on we occasionally hear the background noise of the new baby. When all is quiet in the early hours of the morning we see a figure creeping through the

bodies and out of the cabin – it's Judy. After a while a second figure creeps out – the Indian).

(The lights come up for daylight and Mulligan is first to wake and realize that the Indian's gone)

Mulligan	Jesus! (Shaking Sharpe) Hey! Wake up!
Sharpe	Uh? What's up?
Mulligan	The Indian's gone!
Sharpe	(Jumping up) What? How -? I thought you were covering?
Mulligan	I was. I must have dropped off.
Sharpe	God! You know what this means don't you? We are in serious trouble.
Vanessa	(Stirring) What's wrong?
Sharpe	We've lost the prisoner
Vanessa	No?
Mulligan	I'm sorry but I was so tired
Joe	What's up?
Vanessa	They've lost the Indian.
Tasmin	What?
Joe	The Indian's gone.

Tasmin	Judy's missing as well
Vanessa	Oh no – please God, he hasn't taken her
Joe	Perhaps she's gone to look for him
Tasmin	Do you think?
Joe	(Looking out of the window) Hang on – there's somebody coming
	(The door is forced open with difficulty and Judy appears)
	(They are all looking surprised)
Judy	What's up?
Vanessa	Thank God you're O.K.
Tasmin	We thought –
Vanessa	You'll never guess what's happened
Joe	They've lost the Indian
Judy	No?
Mulligan	You haven't seen any sign of him?
Judy	I'm sorry, can't say I have. I've been out quite a while (To Tasmin) How's the baby?
Tasmin	Fine.

Sharpe	That's it then, that's the end of both our careers
Mulligan	I've said I'm sorry, what more do you want me to say
Sharpe	And what do you think the boss is going to say when she finds out? This is the first time I've ever had to admit losing anybody.
Vanessa	Will you get into much trouble?
Sharpe	And how. (Turning on Mulligan) All you had to do was stay awake for two hours! Two hours - you can't even do that.
Mulligan	I've said I'm sorry – are we going to go after him?
Sharpe	No point now – he'll be long gone
Judy	(Getting up and trying to get some heat out of the stove) Well I'll say one thing, this has been one hell of a trip
Sharpe	You can say that again
Vanessa	It's a New Year I won't forget in a hurry
Judy	(Looking round at the others) You know what, I got to thinking about it last night, we have all human life here (she casts hand around the others) We've had a death and a birth ...

Vanessa   One out and one in.

Cronkheim   (Stirring) What time do you call this?

Judy   It's five a.m.

Cronkheim   I don't remember asking for room service

Judy   Sorry

Cronkheim   (Gets up and tries to warm himself on the stove)

                 I was having a wonderful dream - I was doing
                 really well, just gonna clinch a multi-million
                 dollar deal and the door bursts opens and in
                 comes this all-singing, all-dancing Shirley
                 Temple

Mrs Hooper   (Stirring) I thought you said you were going
                 think before you spoke?

Cronkheim   That was last night.   You were supposed to be
                 asleep

Mrs Hooper   I never sleep

Abigail   What time is it mom?

Mrs Hooper   Five in the morning

Abigail   Is it time to get up?

Mrs Hooper   Not yet. Go back to sleep

Vanessa	I shouldn't bother – they've lost the Indian

Mrs Hooper	(Together) What?
Cronkheim	(Together) What?

Vanessa	You heard

Cronkheim   It don't really surprise me none – he had more brains than the both of them put together.

(Cronkheim goes to look out of the window alongside the others. We see their faces lit up by the morning sunlight from outside)

Cronkheim   Will you look at that - sunrise over the Rockies!

Judy   Yeah, another day, another dollar

Vanessa   Another brand new year ...

(Pause)

Judy   While you were all asleep I've been out doing a little exploring. There's something I need to tell you all.

Cronkheim   Oh yeah? What's that?

Judy   I've found us a road

Cronkheim   (He punches the air and shouts in a loud cowboy drawl) YEEHAH ! (Going towards the door) Well what are we waiting for?

Judy	We need to get everybody ready
Cronkheim	Come on then, let's get going – did you hear that? She's found a road

(General excitement and stirring as they get up and get dressed)

(Mulligan goes to the door of the cabin and finds that it's stuck)

Mulligan	There's only one problem

(Everyone stops and listens)

Judy	What that?
Mulligan	The door won't open.
Judy	You just have to lift it
Mulligan	I've tried lifting it – it's well and truly jammed this time.
Sharpe	Here, let me try

(He tries and fails)

You're right

Joe	We'll just have to get out of a window?
Judy	It isn't that easy, they look like they haven't been opened for years

Vanessa	Just a minute – what's that?
Cronkheim	Not again – that story last night wasn't **real** you know.
Vanessa	There!
Mrs Hooper	(Looking out of the window) Oh my God!
Judy	What is it?
Mrs Hooper	It's the Indian, he's standing there outside
Sharpe	What? Let me see (he goes to look)
	Yeah, it's him all right.
Vanessa	What are we going to do?
Tasmin	What <u>can</u> we do?
Mulligan	(To Sharpe) Are you thinking what I'm thinking?
	(Sharpe nods)
Vanessa	What? What are you thinking?
Mulligan	Do I have to remind you all what he's in for?
Mrs Hooper	You don't think - ?
Mulligan	I don't know what to think
Vanessa	I don't want to be burned alive

Abigail   What do you mean?

Vanessa   He's in for arson.

Mrs Hooper   Oh God, yes.

               (There is a pause then the Indian starts to bang
               slowly and repeatedly on the door getting louder
               each time and they jump with fear with each
               bang. Sharpe and Mulligan draw their weapons
               in readiness before the door finally bursts open to
               show him standing there. He lifts up the limp
               body of a rabbit, looks round them all and says
               with a grin ...)

Sammy   Breakfast !

               (Laughter of relief and general hugs all round as
               the lights go down and the closing music is
               played ... "Come Fly With Me")

NB: With grateful thanks to Arnold R. Shulman, of
               Sedona, Arizona, USA.